SLAUGHTERHOUSE
(*Macello*)

LEGAS

ITALIAN POETRY IN TRANSLATION
VOLUME XVIII

SERIES EDITOR: GAETANO CIPOLLA

Other Volumes Published in this Series:

Ivano Ferrari

SLAUGHTERHOUSE
(*Macello*)

**Introduction and English Translation by
Matteo Gilebbi**

LEGAS

Ivano Ferrari, *Slaughterhouse (Macello),* introduction and translation into English by Matteo Gilebbi.

ISBN 978-1-939693-35-8

Library of Congress Control Number: 2019954797

Acknowledgments

The publisher is grateful to Giulia Di Filippi for the use of her painting "Verso la luce" on the cover from *Opere/Works*, Isernia: Gruppo Petit Prince, 2002.

For information and for orders, write to:

Legas

P. O. Box 149
Mineola, New York
11501, USA

3 Wood Aster Bay
Ottawa, Ontario
K2R 1D3 Canada

Legaspublishing.com

Acknowledgments

First and foremost, I would like to thank Ivano Ferrari, not only for his permission to translate his work, but more importantly for inspiring through his poems a more compassionate relationship between humans and animals. I hope that bringing these poems to a larger English-speaking audience will inspire more people to consider animals "companion species".

This translation project would not have been possible without the inspiration of the many scholars and activists whose work I had the privilege to study: Carol J. Adams, Serenella Iovino, Rosi Braidotti, Marco Maurizi, Bruno Latour, Giorgio Agamben, Richard Ryder, Donna Haraway, Roberto Marchesini, Elena Past, and Stacey Alaimo.

I am also extremely grateful to my mentors Ernesto Livorni and Donatella Marchi, who taught me how to harness the power of poetry.

A special thanks to the The Leslie Center for the Humanities at Dartmouth College for sponsoring this project, to Gaetano Cipolla at Legas Publishing for believing in the importance of this publication, and to Mauro Bersani at Einaudi for giving the right to publish the original text.

I am in great debt to Anthony and Mary Jo Tremmel for their constant support and the incredible work they did proofreading the early draft of my translation. Their suggestions have been invaluable. Also, through their passionate activism against factory farming and concentrated animal feeding operations in Iowa, they have convinced me of the importance of educating the general public about the negative impact of industrial slaughtering.

I am extremely grateful to my wonderful wife Betsy, who in addition to being a brilliant and indispensable proofreader for this book—and for everything I write—is also the source of everything that is joyful in my life.

Finally, this book is dedicated to all the animals encaged and exploited, to all the humans who are fighting for their liberation, and to all the human and nonhuman animals that try to bite back.

Table of Contents/ Indice

Becoming human in the slaughterhouse[1]

Ivano Ferrari (Mantova, b. 1948) is a contemporary Italian poet whose central preoccupation is the complication of being human in a world that treats animals inhumanely. For several years, in the mid-seventies, Ivano Ferrari worked at the municipal slaughterhouse of Mantua, a city in northern Italy where the meat industry has always thrived. Ferrari used the medium of poetry to communicate what he saw and heard in this place where the culture of slaughter is constantly celebrated. He experienced not only the humiliation, suffering, and death of the creatures around him, but also the vitality, sacredness, and redemption of both human and nonhuman lives. His testimony took the form of short poems that share a similar style and structure, collected in two books: *Slaughterhouse* ("Macello"), which includes poems written while employed at the abattoir, but published almost 30 years later, in 2004; and *The Death Wife* ("La Morte Moglie"), published in 2013, which includes poems both rediscovered from his time at the slaughterhouse and more recent poems written after the death of his wife. I have chosen to incorporate the translation of both books into a single volume so readers can directly access the full trajectory of Ferrari's work, which binds poetry to the complex moralities of animal slaughtering, animal rights, worker rights, and the human-animal divide. I hope that making these two books accessible to a larger non-Italian-speaking audience will foster the exploration of speciesism, animal suffering, meat consumption, working conditions in the meatpacking industry, and the human-animal divide through the representation of these issues present in Ferrari's poetry. These translations could also stimulate a discussion about the connection between meat consumption, the livestock industry, and climate change, an important topic for anyone interested in

---

1   This introduction is an updated version of my essay "Witnessing the Slaughter. Human and Nonhuman Animals in Ivano Ferrari's Poetry" published in the volume *Landscapes, Natures, Ecologies: Italy and the Environmental Humanities,* edited by Serenella Iovino, Elena Past, and Enrico Cesaretti (University of Virginia Press, 2018. Pp. 47-56)

the anthropogenic transformation of planet Earth.

The slaughterhouse described by Ferrari is a real space, but, at times, it is also intended as a metaphorical space. In fact, there is a denotative intent in the decision to entitle one of the two collections *Macello*. This is because, in Italian, "macello" means not only "slaughterhouse," but also "mess," "disaster," "massacre," and "chaos." Therefore, it is likely that Ferrari chose "macello" because this word incorporates a reference to both the real and metaphorical mess inside and outside the slaughterhouse. This term conveys the ethical and political message in Ferrari's work and exposes the connection to any physical and metaphorical places where both human and nonhuman animals experience a trauma. In fact, Ferrari considers the slaughterhouse a space that metaphorically refers to other traumatic experiences and to other places of suffering, evoking images of war ("A hog with a slit throat commands me:/ password!), the Holocaust ("no one breathes in the deadly gas"), and class conflict ("tanners, packers and gravediggers,/the working class"). Ferrari, therefore, implies that human violence toward the animal (interspecific violence) is directly related to the violence against other humans (intraspecific violence).

One key cause of interspecific violence is the objectification of the animal: animals must lose their identity and become a commodity before being slaughtered and consumed. Objectification of animals emerges in Ferrari's poetry when he describes his colleagues—"strange creatures" who, by working "like miners," transform the animals into "few nutrients". In the butchers' mind, the animal exists only as nourishment, with its identity being replaced by its function as food. The job of the butcher is thus similar to that of a miner: they both work with inanimate elements. Ferrari works against this objectification process in several of his poems by returning identity to the animal. We see this with the description of the escape of a bull that "wanders on the overpass" in search of freedom, and, instead of being killed in the slaughterhouse, is executed by a firing squad of "cops with machine guns". By escaping the space of the slaughterhouse, the bull also escapes the mechanism of objectification, regaining, in his flight, an identity as a living being. This identity materializes both in the escape, representing the bull's desire to survive the slaughter, and in the moment of death when the animal "whispers something to the flies". This whispering offers a boost of vitality, a desperate desire to communicate, a survival impulse, and, most particularly, a final testimony of suffering. All these acts lead us to recognize the bull not simply as a lifeless piece of meat, but as a single living being able to feel, desire, and suffer.

Ferrari explores in particular how the objectification of the animal reveals a disturbing connection between animal slaughtering and sexual pleasure, a topic examined by scholar and activist Carol Adams in her 1990 book *The Sexual Politics of Meat*, where she exposed in detail the connections between sexism and speciesism. In particular, she provocatively pointed out how commonly sexual metaphors are communicated in the space of animal farming and in slaughterhouses. Here a particular form of fetishism emerges, which equates the consumption of meat to the seduction of women: slaughtering and eroticism overlap. This implies that the oppression of the animal, in addition to being related to speciesism and to the capitalistic mechanism of production and consumption, also concerns a form of sadistic pleasure and sexual perversion. According to Adams, the oppression and exploitation of animals contain the same sexual urges present in the sadistic interaction with women. The slaughter excites the erogenous zones of the human male's logic of dominance. Ferrari's poems bring us even more precise examples of this dynamic, showing us the complexity and depth of the relationship between violence against animals and sexual pleasure, between the slaughterhouse and the brothel. In fact, slaughter connects to eroticism in the poem that opens the book, which emphasizes the carno-sado-pornocentric model as the fundamental ingredient of both Ferrari's poetry and the space of the slaughterhouse. As can be seen in that very first poem, there are spaces in the architecture and organization of the slaughterhouse specifically dedicated to the autoerotic consumption of images of women and animals. The sexual tension that mounts during the slaughtering process must be released in a closet, a secluded place isolated inside the slaughterhouse, indicating that the enjoyment that comes from the submission of the animal/

woman is fully achieved in the dark core of the abattoir's architecture. Significantly, later in the poem a direct connection appears between the naked body of a woman and a cow: "posted on three walls are photos of women/with hairless vaginas/on the other wall the poster of a cow/unveiling with different colors/her delicious cuts." Inside the slaughterhouse, the act of selecting animal parts for consumption corresponds to the selection of female anatomical parts as erotic stimuli. The female body is enjoyed because it has become a selected and dominated piece of meat, and animal flesh is enjoyed because it has become the referent of the domination over the female body. In addition, at the very beginning of that same poem, the combination of violence toward the animal and sexual pleasure materializes in the Italian word "sega", which I have freely translated as "choking the chicken" because "sega" translates as both "saw" and "masturbation." Therefore, the original Italian term evokes the tool ("saw") used to dissect the slaughtered animal and directly connects it to the pleasure ("masturbation") experienced by reducing animals to those discrete pieces similar to the female erotic parts. The saw/masturbation is the end, but also the means, of the domination over the animal in the erotic space of the slaughterhouse.

In many other poems Ferrari calls on the sexual tension present in different stages of slaughtering. For example, animals are often described with precise sensual elements, such as the calves hanging on hooks that "show off", the "limber heifers" smiling, the "elegant heifer", and the "nymphomaniacal bovines". This sexual tension also emerges from the movements of the workers of the slaughterhouse, whose hands, while flaying a bleeding animal, "brine the raw flesh/of a female trainee". Ferrari again aligns slaughtering and the sexual act and emphasizes how the woman is reduced to a scrap of flesh in a butcher shop. Ferrari also bears witness to the sadistic relationship that exists between the human/ruler and animal/victim, such as when he describes a horse as a "faggot dancer" that is sodomized by a butcher with a club and whose death occurs while "offering squirts of organic matter/to his unseducible rapist". At this point, inside the slaughterhouse, the human has taken the identity of a pervert and a molester, and his acts of violence carry a sexual pleasure that, sadistically put into practice in the space of the slaughterhouse, has become an essential element of the animal meat we consume. In addition, it is important to notice that in these poems, the man who rules and rapes the animal remains "unseducible" because the sexual pleasure is sadistic and the depiction of the slaughter is pornographic, leaving no chance for intimacy, however perverse. The distance between human and animal is dilated, and speciesism is strengthened by this perverse enjoyment of the suffering and death of the animal, a pleasure that dramatically connects speciesism to sexism.

Ferrari writes about his own failure in trying to approach the animal in a different, possibly nonviolent way, but even his attempt results in an awkward and embarrassing act of cruelty: "In order to measure the fever of the victim/a thermometer is introduced into the rectum/or (if female) in the vagina/this operation is done without gloves/and it is not hard to insert/together with the instrument a scrap of paper/with poems scribbled earlier". These same poems, written during his time at the abattoir, are composed with the intention of becoming the means for a different relationship with animal otherness, a different approach to the painful condition of the nonhuman animals at the slaughterhouse. But the "poems scribbled" come in contact with the animal through an improper veterinary practice "done without gloves" that recalls more the image of rape and violence than that of intimacy and encounter. Ferrari shows that despite his good intention to witness the slaughter through his poetry, writing itself falls into the category of a brutal act. It seems that interspecies violence, even when reported, is so ingrained in mankind that it is inevitably always put into practice. This is also an interspecific violence that, inside the slaughterhouse, relentlessly produces practices firmly tied to intraspecific violence: his logocentric act of donating poetry to the animal is performed by penetrating its flesh, through a form of rape that makes any communication with the nonhuman impossible. This is the same form of violence that subjugates and violates the female body. Speciesism and sexism are woven together by a poem that, in witnessing the slaughterhouse, is inevitably contaminated by the same violence that this place perpetuates.

The relation between sexism and speciesism connects to another important theme present in Ferrari's work: the practice of animalization. The human is animalized, implicitly or explicitly, via a rhetorical mechanism of power that, assuming the animal condition is inferior, justifies control over those individuals reduced to animals. In his 2004 book *The Open: Man and Animal*, philosopher Giorgio Agamben analyzed this mechanism and presented it as the most typical instrument of modern biopolitical power, renaming this animalization of humans the "anthropological machine," indicating that it is an integral element of the anthropological condition itself. In other words, it comes naturally for the *Homo sapiens* species to control, subjugate, torment, and exterminate other humans by labeling them as inferior species. However, another kind of animalization exists that could be considered positive. This animalization generally occurs in three forms. In its first iteration, it uplifts the human condition to that of the animal, considering the animal superior to man and therefore a model to imitate. The second form instead advocates for unveiling an animal element that has been always present, but hidden, inside the human and aims to return this hidden animality to an anthropological condition considered incomplete when deprived of this untamed and primitive element. The third form considers the animalization of humans the necessary condition for reaching a connection and for building a dialogue with animal otherness; it attempts an interspecific contact in which the human seeks to evolve toward an open-minded embrace of the heterospecific condition.

Ferrari embraces this third form of animalization, a process that reduces the distance between humans and nonhumans and might offset the inhumanity of the slaughterhouse space. In several of his poems, Ferrari describes how the slaughterhouse has become a privileged place for the evolution of inhuman behavior, that is, a lack of understanding for the human and animal condition and an absence of compassion for the suffering that animals experience in the slaughterhouse. This inhumanity often takes the forms of cynical violence: "Striking the beast/with more blows/than it can withstand,/sneering/when it realizes/that it is going to die". At other times, this inhumanity manifests itself as an abyssal

detachment from animal pain directly caused—and witnessed—
by humans: "The dying beast/agonizes alone/because no thing/
happens held in the arms". In several other poems the death of
the animal is an isolated, painful, secret circumstance, pertaining
to the animal alone, with the butcher incapable of demonstrating
any empathy. The animal's death remains unknown or ignored,
accompanied only by the cold inertia of the inhuman: "Having
loaded the weapon/the executioner with greenish eye sockets/
smiles at her (I lie down between little pieces of fat)/he shoots./
The secrets are recomposed/in the extraneousness of death". This
implies that becoming animal inside the slaughterhouse means
resisting inhumanity and seeking empathy and dialogue with the
animal condition. This is a process that goes beyond simple piety,
beyond that "sadness"—Ferrari writes—that "does not prevent
us/from starting the slaughter at seven thirty sharp". Becoming
animal means instead encountering the animal in the space of
its—and our—suffering, in order to be able to stop the mechanism
of inhumanity, of speciesism, of slaughter.

In a 2006 interview with Nicholas Gane, feminist scholar
Donna Haraway raised the possibility of animalization as a new
category of relations based on mutual curiosity that takes place
during the meeting between "mortal, situated, relentlessly relational worlding". Therefore, the process of becoming animal starts
from curiosity among living beings emanating from their own
contingent and relational existence, a post-Heideggerian being
there and being toward death that resets the species distance and
makes the contact between species innate and spontaneous. As a
human species, Haraway insists, we must therefore recognize that
animalization is a form of interspecific relationships historically and
biologically always in place. What we are as humans, and what we
might become, is not acquired in isolation but in the encounter
with the nonhuman, the different, the other, the heterospecific,
an encounter that often takes the form of a collaboration between
what Haraway calls "companion species".

In my view, humans start becoming animals when they recognize this collaboration and work toward making these encoun-
ters possible. This process of animalization brings the human into

contact with those different existential possibilities with which we have always found ourselves in dialogue, through which we also have learned how to relate to the world. Our species can therefore try to escape the cage of anthropocentrism and explore other forms of existence and recognize them as being as dynamic and valid as the human one. In experiencing this animalization, we also find that these forms of existence are not monads but throbbing seeds that are always open to cross-species contamination. Becoming animal means resisting the uncontaminated and lonely inhuman, to get dirty with reality, to get stuck in new worlds, and to compromise our existence by admitting countless others. This is how, according to Haraway, species come together and together transform themselves and evolve, not as heavenly creatures but as terrestrial critters belonging to the mud. And to the blood. Because in actuality, the slaughterhouse is one of the ideal spaces for this encounter between species that allows us to become animal, as it is inside the slaughterhouse that the battle between animalization and inhumanity that abhors cross-species contamination is fought. In the slaughterhouse, a dramatically physical contact between species occurs, a literal skin-to-skin interspecific brush in which the human touches the physicality of animal existence and the reality of animal suffering and death.

Ferrari witnesses this dramatic interspecific encounter, and his poems give us the tools to understand what happens when species meet and become companions in the space of pain and death. First, Ferrari shows us that humans and animals share suffering in the real and metaphorical spilling of the same blood: "Two fingers severed/ almost a metaphor/the blood of one like the other". An incident in which the human animal is a victim becomes the epiphanic episode that transforms the pain into a shared event. The accident reveals the existence of a moment of suffering when we can meet with another species. The awareness of having the same animal blood and the same nervous system capable of feeling the same pain is made banal, a common fact of which the human had been unaware. It is "an instant of stillness, like an afterthought", that for a moment destabilizes human exceptionalism while making us perceive the truth of animal suffering, albeit in relation to ours. Along with suffering comes the "absolute" experience of death that pushes the human toward a particular animalization: the poet takes on the qualities and attitudes of cattle in order to get near a calf and follow him closely during the slaughtering process. This animalization is necessary because the experience of death in the slaughterhouse belongs completely to an animal; therefore, only the animal victim can truly witness this kind of death. Becoming animal is therefore essential to testifying to death in the slaughterhouse: "Tepid, I smell the ass/of the large calf that goes before me/in the race to the absolute". The poet becomes animal by performing animal motions and sharing the same slaughtering space in which we are metaphorically in line with the animal, who goes before us toward the same fate of annihilation. The animal experiences death in front of the human so he can prepare for it. This is why, in his becoming animal, the poet sniffs the calf: he establishes a sensorial communication with the animal who allows him to gaze at death before it is his turn. Our turn. Or the turn of those we love the most, those with whom we have shared our existence. Ferrari suggests a form of animalization that carries a deep emotional and moral impact, especially in the poems written about the illness and death of his wife in the last section of this book. Through portraying the figure of his sick wife becoming animal, Ferrari presents a relationship between human and animal suffering that is even more intimate than in his previous work. So intimate that any interspecific separation fades to give way to the images of humans and animals existing, feeling, suffering, and dying in the same manner.

In the second part of the book, entitled *The Death Wife*, Ferrari's agonizing wife becomes animal because her body belongs to the slaughterhouse as much as an animal body: like these animals, she lies "on a large table about to be eaten", and finally nothing remains of her body "except a meal". In death, her face becomes a "surging snout", and among her human gestures appears the animal trait of "licking the palm of the hand". This is not simple zoomorphism, because there is neither the use of simile nor a metaphorical intent. Instead, the human is biologically animal because it is recognized as an animal as it suffers and dies. What Ferrari saw inside the slaughterhouse he now sees in the hospital: a carcass hanging from a hook is identical to a body lying on a stretcher. These poems confirm the intuition Ferrari had in the slaughterhouse: humans and animals suffer the same pain and experience the same death because they are "companion species." In the hospital and the slaughterhouse, the distance between human and nonhuman animals is eliminated and Ferrari witnesses the presence of a single species made of undifferentiated, sentient beings. We are all this single animal: "As hard as clotted blood/and as soft as calf's marrow/similar am I if not equal". These lines, a perfect synthesis of Ferrari's anti-speciesism, trace the path that crosses similarity and arrives at equality. It is a route that moves through bodily elements shared by humans and animals (the blood and bone marrow), filtered through suffering (the clotted blood). Man or animal, everything is equally body, flesh, sentient matter. And Ferrari constantly tries to communicate this truth via a particularly difficult testimony because it still comes from a butcher, and from a species that has been considering itself the dominant one and that now, self-aware and animalized, breaks out crying, "I am a lamb too".

This animalized poet-butcher now faces the moral necessity of dismantling the slaughterhouse and showing the possibilities of becoming animal to the rest of the slaughterers and meat eaters. Ferrari sketches this new phase by forming hypotheses and questions: "If I broke down the wall of flesh/and hanging from the hook I smiled/what would he say who is paid to dismember/the stamper of tongues/what label would they put on me/how many organs would they discard/and would the vet think panta rei?". The final passage of becoming animal is this hypothetical self-replacing of the animal victim, a sacrifice full of Christological tensions that, by transforming the slaughterhouse into the space of human slaughter, may cause it to short-circuit. It might. Ferrari does not anticipate the consequences of this hypothetical self-sacrifice of becoming animal; he only questions. The mechanisms of the slaughterhouse, of speciesism, of the control over the animal, and of its eroto-capitalistic transformation into an object seem so ingrained in the practices of our species that they may never be called into question, not even in the face of the human becoming animal. The anthropological machine always uses human animalization as a mechanism of domination: it would become even easier to slaughter fellow humans when they voluntarily replace animals. What remains, then, of Ferrari's poetry is the affirmation that a different animalization, while unlikely, is possible—an animalization realized, through a convergence between humans and animals who understand and share the same, universal suffering. With these poems, Ferrari begins the search for an alternative way of becoming animal, that is, the chance to approach an understanding of the heterospecific in a space built on the solidarity of pain. His work testifies that in this space, a space that emerges inside the slaughterhouse, humans can recognize their sadistic practices of control, transcend their inhumanity, and find empathy with fellow human and nonhuman animals.

SLAUGHTERHOUSE
(*Macello*)

Slaughterhouse

To Cesare Cancellieri

The closet at the bottom of the locker room
is where you choke the chicken
posted on three walls are photos of women
with hairless vaginas
on the other wall the poster of a cow
unveiling with different colors
her delicious cuts.

My polished and sad skin
the smooth heart
the bruised complexion
well, I am the one
who determines the edibility
of your miasmatic foods.

All of them in a row
naked
slightly soiled with manure
they wait to be perfected
while stammering objections
the most resourceful sodomizes the buddy he follows
the scream that rises is only a prospect
the stunbolt gun restrains the scandal
there are dutch belted cows
calves
and a few horses.

Macello

A Cesare Cancellieri

Lo stanzino in fondo allo spogliatoio
è detto delle seghe
affisse a tre pareti foto di donne
dalla vagina glabra
nell'altra il manifesto di una vacca
che svela con differenti colori
i suoi tagli prelibati.

La mia pelle ripulita e triste
il cuore glabro
il colorito bluastro
bene, io sono quello
che stabilisce la commestibilità
dei vostri miasmatici cibi.

Tutti in fila
nudi
appena sporchi di letame
attendono la perfezione
balbettando proteste
il più intraprendente sodomizza il compagno davanti
l'urlo che si alza è solo un anticipo
la rivoltella a pressione frena lo scandalo
ci sono vacche olandesi
torelli
e qualche cavallo.

The first day
something soggy suddenly
clutches my neck
like a scarf
someone had thrown at me
a never-ending bull penis.

Where will he hide the tears?
If the question hangs on the smashed
skull of a colt
I fade while laboring verses
while suffering animals and things.

Black,
marked with infamy
loud and slender.
I make of him pieces
minutiae of a broken horse
to avenge my daughter
(to bring them closer to the gun
they call them "Brave Stallion").

The hand will shoot
it is good to keep in mind
that the wrist is to be held up,
an eye will come off
(big beast double charge)
on the ground, the harvest moon.

Il primo giorno
d'un tratto il molliccio
mi avvinghia il collo
come una sciarpa
qualcuno mi aveva lanciato
un interminabile pene di toro.

Dove nasconderà le lacrime?
Se la domanda pende sul cranio
sfondato di un puledro
sfumo affannando versi
subendo animali e cose.

Nero,
macchiato di infamia
rumoroso e snello.
Ne faccio pezzetti
minuzie di cavallo spezzato
per vendicare mia figlia
(per farli avvicinare alla pistola
li chiamano "Furia").

La mano farà fuoco
è bene ricordare
di sostenere il polso,
si staccherà un occhio
(bestia grossa doppia carica)
per terra, il plenilunio.

There is a calf that is still breathing
the shot did not break the skull
whoever made the mistake grabs the neck
squeezes the shape
the eyeballs of the bovine dance
to the rhythm of the hoist.

"In cattle
because of the strong development of the frontal sinuses
the region
at which the brain can be directly hit
is very narrow
at least with the so-called sledgehammer technique"
and in addition
"importantly live cattle must not
make contact with slaughtered beef".

The dead flesh lives again
in its great misery
with the wind that brings back scents
to an extended order.
The dead flesh is embroidered
by those sinuous beings
that others call larvae.

C'è un vitello che respira ancora
il colpo non ha sfondato il cranio
chi ha sbagliato gli afferra il collo
stringe la forma
i globi degli occhi bovini ballano
al ritmo del paranco.

"Nei bovini
per il forte sviluppo dei seni frontali
è ristrettissima la regione
attraverso la quale si può immediatamente
colpire il cervello
almeno con la tecnica detta della mazza"
e ancora
"evitare in modo particolare che il bestiame vivo
si incontri con le carni macellate".

La carne morta rivive
nella sua grande miseria
col vento che riporta gli odori
ad un ordine sparso.
La carne morta è ricamata
da quelle sinuose presenze
che gli altri chiamano larve.

Worms
that combusted surrender
to the blond-o'-the-wisp of the summer
youngsters with feeble tenacity
sparks in this darkness.

Tireless homicides
between incense and carcasses bartered
with the anticipated corruption of dreams,
while I evaporate (de-greasing phase)
I cede the words:
show me my death
so that I could know what you all live for.

I stick fingers into the hard nostrils
of the decapitated bull
I seek intimacy and mindset
in that crippled vigor
when I could have hands
filled with breasts.

From the necrobiotic vapor
the osmosis
called by an archeological anxiety.
Tepid, I smell the ass
of the large calf that goes before me
in the race to the absolute.

Vermi
che combusti cedono
al biondo fatuo dell'estate
giovani dalla tenacia molle
scintille in questo buio.

Omicidi instancabili
tra incenso e carogne barattate
con l'attesa corruzione dei sogni,
mentre evaporo (sgrassaggio)
cedo le parole:
dimostratemi la mia morte
che conosca ciò per cui vivete.

Ficco dita nelle narici dure
del toro decapitato
cerco intimità e pensiero
in quel vigore moncato
quando potrei avere colme
le mani di mammelle.

Dal vapore necrobiotico
l'osmosi
chiamata da una archeologica ansia.
Tiepido, annuso il culo
del grosso vitello che mi precede
nella corsa verso l'assoluto.

Memories (fired)
besiege the big head of an old cow
in the mouth
the taste is what at night
provokes in me guilt
vomited with wine.
(Clouds of blood draw near
where the city conspires).

One hundred hearts
one hundred tongues
one hundred tails
one hundred farts
gaseous greatness
for my art.

I hide in the cage and wait
for the fatigue to glisten men's gazes
even if tears are not needed
to wash the entrails.
Then I lift the blade truncating
air, odor and remorse
that run down the drain with the bull's head
and its dumb and endless eyes.

I ricordi (sparati)
assediano il testone di una vecchia vacca
nella bocca
il sapore è quello che di notte
mi procura il senso di colpa
vomitato col vino.
(Nuvole di sangue si avvicinano
dove cospira la città).

Cento cuori
cento lingue
cento code
cento peti
gassosa grandezza
per la mia arte.

Mi nascondo nella gabbia e aspetto
che la stanchezza lucidi gli sguardi degli uomini
anche se le lacrime non servono
a lavare i budelli.
Poi alzo la falza troncando
aria, odori e pentimenti
che scendono nello scarico con la testa del toro
dagli occhi infiniti e beoti.

There is a moment during the slaughter,
when the lifting mechanism
raises the hock by which the animal hangs,
where the sacrifice of the crucifixion continues to occur
including St. Longinus with the hooked pole
that stabilizes the body for easier shredding.

The carnivorous hierarchies
are covered by smocks
in the white desert
they carve with blunt knives
while the mortifying adventure begins
I glimpse the pliant line
that sublimates the protest
of the skinniest horse.
Like miners
strange creatures
covered by blue cloth (blackened by blood)
extract few nutrients
from their weighed down heads.

Clouds that burst
like badly dug dens
scar the city
like black drops
cremated a laboratory lamb
stench of sky.

C'è un momento della macellazione,
quando l'organo di sollevamento
solleva il gambare a cui è appeso l'animale,
in cui si ripete il sacrificio della crocifissione
compreso un S. Longino con pertica uncinata
che stabilizza il corpo per meglio tagliuzzare.

Le carnivore gerarchie
si coprono col camice
nel deserto bianco
affettano da coltelli sdentati
mentre inizia l'umiliante avventura
intravedo l'arrendevole teoria
che sublima la protesta
del più magro fra i cavalli.
Come minatori
strane creature
coperte da tela blu (annerita dal sangue)
estraggono parchi nutrimenti
dalle loro teste appesantite.

Nuvole che scoppiano
come tane malscavate
borchiano la città
come gocce nere
cremato un agnello da esperimento
fetore di cielo.

A secret fills the hairy temples
of a young heifer
and the childish eyes guard it
with a few tears,
a wrinkled crease in her smile
before dying
and she is the only one who doesn't fill with sound
the space of death.
She sees me (I mark the gender on the chart)
and I complicitly confirm the message.
Having loaded the weapon
the executioner with greenish eye sockets
smiles at her (I lie down between little pieces of fat)
he shoots.
The secrets are recomposed
in the extraneousness of death.

Rotund cats
in the order of things
here with us
in continuous cycle,
better than rabbits
if one can
get rid of the gamy taste,
sometimes they lose
their head like all
edible subjects.

Un segreto riempie le tempie pelose
di una giovane manza
e gli occhi infantili lo custodiscono
con qualche lacrima,
una piega rugosa nel suo sorriso
prima di morire
ed è l'unica a non riempire di suoni
lo spazio della morte.
Mi vede (segno il sesso sulla tabella)
e confermo complice il messaggio.
Caricata l'arma
il boia dalle orbite verdastre
gli sorride (giaccio tra pezzetti di grasso)
spara.
I segreti si ricompongono
nella estraneità della morte.

Gatti tondi
nell'ordine delle cose
qui da noi
che siamo in ciclo,
meglio dei conigli
se si riesce
a togliere il selvatico,
delle volte perdono
la testa come tutti
i soggetti commestibili.

An escaped black bull
wanders on the overpass
scaring the traffic,
we chase him
branding knives
stun rods and beers
he runs stops returns
cops with machine guns arrive,
now he lies on a thin veil of grass
and whispers something to the flies.

Shit is colorful
creative
gratifying (a cart every three large bowels)
it is noisy, mellow, intriguing
chilly
when it stubbornly gets stuck in the grills of the drain
it is docile, it is the hay of childhood memories
(we dump it in a concrete tank)
it is reddish when it warns you of some pain
like an ulcer in the ass;
shit (the big tank must be emptied every now and then)
protects my intimacy and yours
stripped
of any prejudice.

When they cut off the light
death put itself back together
to reappear immediately afterwards
more vivid, more virgin.

È fuggito un toro nero
erra sul cavalcavia
impaurendo il traffico,
lo rincorriamo
impugnando coltelli
bastoni elettrici e birre
corre si ferma torna
arrivano i carabinieri coi mitra,
ora è steso su un velo d'erba
e sussurra qualcosa alle mosche.

La merda è colorata
creativa
gratificante (ogni tre ventroni un carretto)
è rumorosa, suadente, intrigante
gelida
quando si ammucchia ostinata nelle grate dello scarico
è docile, è fieno dei ricordi d'infanzia
(la vuotiamo in una vasca di cemento)
è rossastra quando ti avvisa di qualche dolore
come un ulcera al culo;
la merda (la grande vasca va svuotata ogni tanto)
protegge la mia intimità e la vostra
svestita
da qualsiasi pregiudizio.

Quando hanno tolto la luce
la morte si è ricomposta
per apparire subito dopo
più nitida, più vergine.

My ghost
is in a bad mood.
I trade his screaming captivity
with a bag of pink
lungs (streaked with purple)
leftovers
of beastly certainties.

Rubbery glands
filthy remains of tails
mastitis with a heart engraved
caged muses ready
like beasts.

Few words
uttered regrets damage the knives
it is the tacit agreement that unites us
when the boot of a worker
crushes the uterus ripped from a mature cow.
Fails to save us the following and predictable
belch of embarrassment.

*Il mio fantasma
è di cattivo umore.
Scambio l'urlata sua prigionia
con un sacchetto di polmoni
rosa (striati di viola)
rimasugli
di certezze bestiali.*

*Ghiandole gommose
resti stercolosi di code
mastiti con inciso un cuore
muse pronte in gabbia
come bestie.*

*Poche parole
i pentimenti discorsivi danneggiano i coltelli
è il tacito accordo che ci unisce
quando lo stivale di un addetto
schiaccia l'utero strappato a una bovina matura.
Né ci salva il successivo e scontato
rutto di imbarazzo.*

A heifer amazed at being alive
looks at us who ignore her,
dozens of hanging sisters show off,
still breathing she feels lonely and ugly
but there are no more hoists left
and the refrigerating rooms are full,
she rolls her sweet eyes around
if it is a break or a truce nobody senses
she retracts, screams and slips on the blood
it rains plasma for a little, and finally
a hoist opens up.

The prophets of wicked sanitation
do not interest us
we are cast on a miasmatic path
(sadness does not prevent us
from starting the slaughter at seven thirty sharp).

Today death is maternal
little calves plagued by aphthae
run tenderly toward her.

Two fingers severed
almost a metaphor
the blood of one like the other
the cussing, the iodine.
An instant of stillness, like an afterthought
then the mandate of the pitchfork
that searches for justice in the sphincters of a heifer.

Una vitella stupita d'esser viva
guarda noi che la ignoriamo,
decine di sorelle appese si pavoneggiano,
si sente sola e brutta a respirare
ma non ci sono più paranchi
e le celle frigorifere sono colme,
rotea intorno lo sguardo suo più dolce
se è pausa o tregua nessuno raccoglie
si gonfia, lancia un grido e scivola sul sangue
piove plasma per un poco e finalmente
si libera un paranco.

I propagatori di inique nettezze
non ci interessano
siamo proiettati su di un miasmatico percorso
(la tristezza non ci impedisce
di iniziare la macellazione alle sette e trenta precise).

Oggi la morte è materna
vitellini impestati dall'afta
le corrono incontro affettuosi.

Due dita tagliate di netto
quasi una metafora
il sangue uguale all'altro
le bestemmie, lo iodio.
Un attimo di immobilità, come un ripensamento
poi la delega al forcone
che cerca giustizia tra gli sfinteri di una manzarda.

A long, unbearable delay.
Then the noise of the trucks
the screams of the drivers
the last prayers of the beasts.
The resumption of life the reappearance of gibbets
guns, scythes, knives.

Hate also hides
in the wandering martyrdom
of that lot of black bulls
where the attributes of reason
are as useless
as the duty of killing them.

Day of joy in the horror
great bonfire. Crackling turmoil
tires, desks, bloody paws
a storm of sparks as June trickles
with calf heads, canine profiles, and piglets.
In the savory smoke bluish shadows bang
against the widowed ceiling of the sky
objects and animals in the fire that leaves behind
just a herd of eyes lynched on the snouts.

Irritated by the triumphalism of blood
and sated by nature
I roll my eyes in a circle
aesthetically silent
in front of
the failure of the filtration system.

Un lungo, insopportabile ritardo.
Poi il rumore dei camion
le urla degli autisti
le ultime preghiere delle bestie.
Ricomincia la vita appaiono le forche
le pistole, le falze, i coltelli.

L'odio si nasconde anche
nello svolazzante martirio
di quella partita di tori neri
dove gli attributi della ragione
sono vani
come il dovere di ammazzarli.

Giorno di gioia nell'obbrobrio
gran falò. Tumulto crepitante
copertoni, scrivanie, zampe sanguinanti
bufera di faville mentre cola giugno
con testine di vitello, profile canini e giovani porci.
Nel fumo saporoso ombre bluastre cocciano
contro il soffitto vedovile del cielo
oggetti e animali nel fuoco che risparmia
solo un branco di occhi impiccati ai musi.

Irritato dal trionfalismo del sangue
e sazio di natura
roteo gli occhi a cerchio
esteticamente silenzioso
di fronte
all'impotenza dei depuratori.

I swing attached to the beast
with eyes on the nests where
withered birds demand meat,
a cow's tongue replaces the moon
a few drops of blood
try to counter the backflow
of colorless waves.
A hog with a slit throat commands me:
password!

The old cow had
the twilight in her womb
dull guts and a gray vagina,
they loaded her on a military truck.

Almost asleep I watch
herds of young mice
attack the rotten flesh,
fat and unhurried
they dissect the divine
starting from the bottom.
The logic of extermination
in the tiny greedy bites
that rip thoughts apart.

In the silence made flesh,
the light seeps through the carcasses
but with a shiver escapes.

Dondolo aggrappato alla bestia
con gli occhi sui nidi dove
rattrappiti volatili chiedono carne,
una lingua di vacca sostituisce la luna
alcune gocce di sangue
provano a contrastare il riflusso
di onde senza colore.
Un porco sgozzato mi intima:
parola d'ordine!

L'anziana vacca aveva
il crepuscolo nel ventre
budelli spenti e la vagina grigia,
l'hanno caricata su un camion militare.

Quasi dormendo osservo
mandrie di giovani topi
avventarsi sulla carne guasta,
grassi e senza fretta
sezionano il divino
muovendo dal fondo.
La logica di sterminio
nei piccoli morsi golosi
con cui sbranano i pensieri.

Nel silenzio di carne,
passa luce dalle carcasse
ma in un brivido fugge.

The knives mate
in the monotonous color of blood
tired of the games of hemorrhagic gods
not even the exciting and deep tunic (pale mucous membrane)
can recharge them with joy
inflamed by widespread emphysema
they lie face down (and clean)
in the spherical can of time.

In the waiting room
a spotted calf
and a curvy heifer
will still have the night
to sniff promises
as of tomorrow eternal.

For the problems of the soul
the storage room:
with the bloodless quarters and halves
the gender tags
the destination label
the conscious tip-off of the scale.
We confess by stepping on discarded kidneys
bone splinters and layers of fat.
Freer, later, we devour
slices of raw meat (from the finest cuts)
just a little salt
and much devotion.

I coltelli si accoppiano
nel monotono colore del sangue
stanchi dei giochi di emorragiche divinità
nemmeno l'esaltante e profonda tunica (pallida mucosa)
può ricaricarli di gioia
infiammati dai diffusi enfisemi
giacciono prostrate (e ripuliti)
nel rotondo bidone del tempo.

Nella stanza d'attesa
un vitellone chiazzato
e una tornita manzarda
avranno ancora la notte
per annusarsi promesse
da domani eterne.

Per i problemi dell'anima
la sala stoccaggio:
coi quarti e le mezzene senza sangue
i cartellini del sesso
l'etichetta di destinazione
la delazione cosciente della bilancia.
Ci si confessa pestando reni di scarto
schegge d'ossa e strati di grasso.
Più liberi, dopo, divoriamo
fettine di carne cruda (dei quarti più belli)
appena un po' di sale
e tanta devozione.

The bled animal
has the feet removed
the head
the intestines
then flayed
by the same hands
that brine the raw flesh
of a female trainee.

Winged men (to be punctual)
galloping while barely moving their lips
the primordial features
the stomachs dilated by blood
the hands clinging to an inferior evil
with ravaging shrewdness
of some electric saw,
we will not be avenged!

These big heads
that dangle
like wilted petals
I'll caress them
in the washing troughs.

L'animale dissanguato
viene privato dei piedi
della testa
degli intestini
quindi scorticato
dalle stesse mani
che acconciano la carne viva
di una praticante.

Uomini alati (per puntualità)
al galoppo muovendo appena le labbra
i lineamenti primordiali
gli stomaci dilatati dal sangue
le mani aggrappate ad un infimo male
con l'astuzia sventrante
di qualche sega elettrica,
non saremo vendicati!

Questi grossi zucconi
che ciondolano
come petali appassiti
li accarezzerò
nei truogoli di lavaggio.

Those wings with which
the huge bovines
are reborn lightweight and incomprehensible
those aligned brains
imprisoned by immutable colors
where surely hides
the logic of some god
those screams
which call to order the porters
who handle
the heaviest of the problems.

But why in the morning
to have breakfast
we always choose the room
next to the handling of viscera
couldn't we have it in the lab
in the offices or even in the restrooms,
perhaps the cleanest place,
let's have it where we store
in the weigh station
at the pavilion of the foreign meats
why the erudite fixation
of the petit-déjeuner sur la merde?

Quelle ali con cui
gli enormi bovini
rinascono leggeri e incomprensibili
quelle cervella allineate
prigioniere di colori immutabili
dove certamente si nasconde
la ragione di qualche divinità
quell'urlo
che richiama all'ordine i facchini
che si accollano
i più pesanti fra i problemi.

Ma perché alla mattina
per fare colazione
si sceglie sempre la stanza
a fianco della tripperia
non potremmo farla nel laboratorio
negli uffici o anche nei cessi,
il luogo forse più pulito,
facciamola dove stocchiamo
nella guardiola della pesa
al padiglione carni foranee
perché la colta fissazione
del petit-déjeuner sur la merde?

Between a chronically decomposed identity
and the moist stammering of water (spraying)
trembles the interstice
that passing through the rubbery ducts of the esophagus
whitened by the fasting of verbs
paves my conscience revealing to me that:
the presence of small air bubbles
of different volumes
(usually from a millet seed to a pea)
aligned in series
in the interglobular connective septa
are often found under the pleurae.

From an intestine (of a bull)
dilated and wrinkled
emanate obsessive sounds
like words
that infect the air (I use gloves)
so that a lacerating silence
fills the great room
where death is performed.

From the tank of boiling water
a huge pig emerges
white as a ghost
swinging lewd until
from the window the sun
ignites tons of light.

Tra un'identità decomposta cronicamente
e l'umido balbettare dell'acqua (a getto)
freme l'interstizio
che nell'attraversare i tubi gommosi dell'esofago
sbiancato dal digiunare dei verbi
mi spiana la coscienza rivelandomi che:
la presenza di bollicine d'aria
di vario volume
(in genere da un grano di miglio ad un pisello)
disposte in linea serliata
nei setti connettivi interglobulari
si trovano sovente sotto la pleura.

Da un intestino (di toro)
dilatato e grinzoso
escono suoni ossessivi
come parole
che appestano l'aria (uso i guanti)
cosí che un lacerante silenzio
riempie la grande sala
dove si esibisce la morte.

Dalla vasca d'acqua bollente
emerge un enorme maiale
bianco come uno spettro
che oscilla impudico fino a quando
dal finestrone il sole
accende quintali di luce.

Buffoons armed
with the dull frills of cruelty
warriors in everything except in appearance
they face the nihil of a crippled bovine
that on its back has branded the "U"
of urgency.

They call them rebels
they are the thoughts that cross
the borders of the afternoon cleaning
they call them rebels
because they reject the graves
where desires are aligned
with the scrap (fat, bones, uteri)
that fills up the trenches
inside which the veterans resist.

Entire families gutted
today
Monday of intense slaughter.
A cow gave birth to a calf
in his eyes the fear of being born
the hole in the middle our contribution
to calm him down.

Cialtroni armati
degli orpelli blandi della crudeltà
guerrieri in tutto fuorché nei lineamenti
affrontano il nihil di un bovino zoppo
che sul groppone ha impresso la "U"
di urgenza.

Li chiamano ribelli
sono i pensieri che valicano
i confini delle pulizie pomeridiane
li chiamani ribelli
perché rifiutano i sepolcri
in cui i desideri sono allineati
con lo scarto (grasso, ossa, uteri)
che va a riempire le trincee
dentro cui i veterani si difendono.

Sventrate intere famiglie
oggi
lunedì di intensa macellazione.
Una vacca ha partorito un vitello
negli occhi la paura di nascere
il foro in mezzo il nostro contributo
a tranquillizzarlo.

Strike
no one slaughters
no one skins
no one dismembers
no one picks up shit
no one breathes in the deadly gas
strike
against Augusto Pinochet
the butcher.

They confront
parenchymal generations
vascular
myocardial (steatosis)
hyaline
amyloid
but without pleasure:
the knives
methodical and obtuse
earn the privilege
of a practice
sharp only in appearance.

Sciopero
non si macella
non si scuoia
non si squarta
non si raccoglie merda
non si annusa il gas della morte
sciopero
contro Augusto Pinochet
il macellaio.

Affrontano
generazioni parenchimatose
vascolari
miocardiche (steatosi)
jaline
amiloidi
ma senza piacere:
i coltelli
metodici e ottusi
si guadagnano il privilegio
di una pratica
solo in apparenza tagliente.

It's a purulent cystitis.
On the udders flows
yellowish blood
nourishment that catches me
naked in the locker rooms
curdled and pink milk
no child's thought clings to it
no swing will happily sway,
for this
evidently just for this
I refuse to clean
the little stream that joyously
runs to infect.

The facial expression of the throat slitter
has no clear origin
it is an obsessive process of human-kind,
inevitably my hands tremble
when I light him a cigarette.

I saw the butcher's wife
(halves and quarters)
a stocky brunette
with lazy sensual movements
wrapped in a strong scent of rosemary.

È una cistite purulenta.
Sulle mammelle scorre
il sangue giallastro
nutrimento che mi coglie
nudo negli spogliatoi
latte raggrumato e rosa
nessun pensiero di bimbo vi si aggrappa
nessuna altalena dondolerà felice,
per questo
solo per questo evidentemente
mi rifiuto di pulire
il piccolo torrente che gioiosamente
corre ad infettare.

La mimica facciale di chi sgozza
non ha un'origine definita
è un processo ossessivo di tipo umano,
inevitabile che mi tremino le mani
quando gli accendo una sigaretta.

Ho visto la moglie di chi squarta
(mezzene e quarti)
è una signora tozza e bruna
con movenze pigre e sensuali
avvolta in un forte profumo di rosmarino.

The scrawny calves
swing without the joy
of those who hanged themselves for love
(the skinner checks the number)
the scrawny calves smell of milk.
I vomit checking the pulse of their butcher.

Butchers against porters
ball the hard heart of the bull
slippery field
posts two empty hoists
referee a health inspector.

The unnatural capsizes
in the midday break.
The cautious swinging of half-carcasses
with the aseptic rhetoric of the cleaned floor
give emphasis to an unfaithful matter
to the small leaks of nature.

I vitelli rachitici
dondolano senza la gioia
degli impiccati per amore
(chi scuoia controlla il numero)
i vitelli rachitici sanno anche di latte.
Vomito controllando il polso di chi li squarta.

Macellatori contro facchini
palla il cuore sodo del toro
terreno scivoloso
pali due paranchi vuoti
arbitra un vigile sanitario.

L'innaturale naufraga
nella pausa di mezzogiorno.
L'oscillare cauto delle mezzene
con l'asettica retorica del pavimento ripulito
danno risalto a una materia infedele
alle piccolo fughe della natura.

Truth with huge fat lips
(pieces of bone and cooled gushes of blood
follow the anxiety of my broom)
serrated words as if ifs had a soul
dozens of tongues hang
already corrupted by the dirty purple
of my power,
this is the hour when death
stands up and checks the beats
of the organs that escaped her,
of the nerves that slacken,
of the last timid beasts
that make me swallow emotions.

The first thing out of the mouth
of an animal that is shot
is a thick whitish foam
there are days when the amount of drool
fills the cage
the blood duct
the cattle passageway
the workstation where the labels are attached
and the lab and the locker rooms and the offices
and the teak crucifix.

At a few hundred meters
past the fresh shape of the lawn
and after houses with dull eyes
the cemetery for humans is located
where there is meat that does not feed.

Verità dai grossi labbroni carnosi
(pezzi di ossa e fiotti raffreddati di sangue
seguono l'ansia della mia scopa)
parole dentate come se i se avessero l'anima
decine di lingue penzolano
ormai corrotte dal viola sporco
del mio potere,
è l'ora in cui la morte
si alza in piedi e controlla i battiti
degli organi che le sono sfuggiti,
dei nervi che si distendono,
delle ultime bestie timide
che mi fanno ingoiare emozioni.

La prima cosa che esce dalla bocca
di un animale sparato
è una schiuma biancastra e spessa
vi sono giorni in cui la quantità di bava
riempie la gabbia
la canaletta del sangue
il camminamento dei bovini
la postazione in cui si attaccano le etichette
e il laboratorio e gli spogliatoi e gli uffici
e il crocefisso in teck.

A qualche centinaio di metri
passata la forma fresca del prato
e dopo case dagli occhi spenti
si trova il cimitero degli umani
dove c'è carne che non sfama.

The water in the eyes
has no power
on the gray crusts of the wall
no strength is needed,
this is enough to give
substance to the identity
we'll talk later
of the adult reason for doubt
(when I'll take off my boots).

With hands in the belly
of a crippled filly,
inside her shit there are tapeworms
strands of chive
crimson seeds of berries
and a piece of streaked glass,
in that warm silence of slime
there is hubris.

I saw shadows crawling
kneaded with the human
and the daggers disgracing the revenge;
I saw god trampling on an apostle
to arrive later at the cage
and the halo
used as baling wire
to convince a young bull to become a saint.

L'acqua degli occhi
non ha potere
sulle croste grigie del muro
né serve la forza,
basta questo per dare
sostanza all'identità
parleremo poi
della ragione adulta del dubbio
(quando mi sarò tolto gli stivali).

Con le mani nel ventre
di una puledra zoppa,
dentro la sua merda ci sono tenie
fili d'erba cipollina
chicchi purpurei di bacche
e un pezzetto di vetro screziato,
in quel caldo silenzio di melma
c'è superbia.

Ho visto strisciare ombre
impastate di umano
e i pugnali disonorare la vendetta;
ho visto dio calpestare un apostolo
per arrivare dopo alla gabbia
e l'aureola
usata come filo di ferro
per convincere un giovane toro a farsi santo.

The splits of the mute horse
faggot dancer that earlier
relished the hayfork handle
and now slips gracefully to the ground
offering squirts of organic matter
to his unseducible rapist.

In nymphomaniacal bovines
have been seen ovaries
soaked in seriousness
it is unclear
due to the lack of a histological test
whether it is a genuine
or an inflammatory edema
or if this is caused
by a questionable notion
of freedom.

In order to measure the fever of the victim
a thermometer is introduced into the rectum
or (if female) in the vagina
this operation is done without gloves
and it is not hard to insert
together with the instrument a scrap of paper
with poems scribbled earlier.

La spaccata del cavallo muto
ballerino culattone che prima
ha goduto del manico di forca
e ora scivola con grazia a terra
offrendo schizzi organici
al suo inseducibile violentatore.

In bovine ninfomani
sono state viste ovaie
imbibite di seriosità
è dubbio
mancando un esame istologico
se si tratti di edema genuino
o infiammatorio
oppure se ciò si deve
ad un equivoco concetto
di libertà.

Per provare la febbre al macellando
si introduce un termometro nel retto
o a scelta (se femmina) nella vagina
questa operazione è fatta senza guanti
e non si fatica ad infilare
assieme allo strumento un bigliettino
di versi scarabocchiati prima.

It is I who with lips like suction cups
pastes my mouth
to the vagina of the huge cow
sucking its odorous mysteries
and its melancholic despair
I
who growling with pleasure
collect its becoming
other from me.

Not only
but actually
it is almost an angel
that degenerates
continuously
spying on me from the top of a hook
unsteady, also, because of the weight.

Between the evisceration room
and the incinerator
grow some flowers
daisies evacuated by the soil
dandelions looking like spit
poppies considerably pale.

Sono io che con labbra a ventosa
incollo la bocca
alla vagina dell'enorme vacca
succhiandone i misteri odorosi
e la malinconica disperazione
io
che ringhiando di piacere
raccolgo il suo divenire
altro da me.

Non solo
anzi
è quasi un angelo
ciò che degenera
senza risparmio
spiandomi dall'alto di un gancio
melfermo, anche, per via del peso.

Tra il fecaio
e l'inceneritore
crescono dei fiori
margherite evacuate dalla terra
soffioni che sembrano sputi
papaveri notevolmente pallidi.

They fill the intestines with water
while singing a love song
anxiety has the breath of the purifiers
cigarettes limit the stress
intestines swell
they squeeze the hall and the throat (gut room)
they grow
they come out to warm up the becoming
they capture
then they go back to kneel
emptied
under the shadow of a tiny
bovine fetus.

The curious audience of flies
praises the opulence that
shits on the cosmos at every hour
on this defecatory Thursday.
Because of an epidemic, they say, there are
still one hundred animals to disembowel.

It is Good Friday but without
the wandering of spring,
already generous with resurrections
the blood still freezes
filling the breaths with glares
and the beasts are too heavy
to get off the cross.

Riempiono di acqua i budelli
cantando una canzone d'amore
l'ansia ha il respiro dei depuratori
le sigarette limitano gli affanni
i budelli si gonfiano
stringono lo stanzone e la gola (tripperia)
crescono
escono a riscaldare il divenire
catturano
poi ritornano ad inginocchiarsi
svuotati
sotto l'ombra di un piccolo
feto bovino.

La curiosa platea delle mosche
inneggia all'opulenza con cui
s'immerda il cosmo ad ogni ora
in questo giovedì defecatore.
Per un'epidemia, dicono, ci sono
ancora cento bestie da sventrare.

È venerdì santo ma senza
la primaverile viandanza,
già prodiga di resurrezioni
il sangue ancora ghiaccia
riempiendo i fiati di bagliori
e le bestie sono troppo pesanti
per scendere dalla croce.

No purple decorations
the crosses covered by dirty overalls
the incense deodorizes other churches,
the candles don't burn
only horse fat with anthrax
and yet the sanctity of the sacrifice
envelops every space of the carnage
tamed muscles, wasted nerves
certainly too much for a god
with his nose in the air.

We are not authorized
for the slaughtering of sheep
but sometimes from the truck
a lamb descends
they jump on it in two
they cover it with a dark tarp
they drag the sheep into the gut room
and there they strangle it with white rope
afterwards, one chooses to lift it
the other cuts the little entrails in half
that spread without the need for space,
the one who holds the creature sweats a lot
the other skins and cuts more composed.

Niente addobbi viola
le croci coperte dalle tute sporche
l'incenso deodora altre chiese,
non bruciano candele
solo grasso di cavalli col carbonchio
eppure la santità del sacrificio
avvolge ogni spazio del carnaio
muscoli domati, nervi di scarto
certamente troppo per un dio
con la puzza al naso.

Non siamo abilitati
alla macellazione ovina
ma qualche volta dal camion
scende un agnello
gli si avventano addosso in due
lo coprono con tela scura
trascinano l'ovino in tripperia
e lì con corde bianche lo strangolano
dopo, uno si incarica di sollevarlo
l'altro incide a metà i viscerini
che si spargono senza necessità di spazio,
quello che tiene la bestiola suda molto
l'altro scortica e taglia più composto.

Limber heifers smile
taking as comedic the screams
of those who put them in line to die
the profile itself of that laughing
is made of spontaneous scenes
clouds designed to seem distant
the dark curtain of half-carcasses
and extras electrified by the spasm
of the director.

A dog with labored breathing arrives
who finishes him?
Nobody comes forward and the beast
throws whimpers and asks for wounds
from a pocket someone pulls out the billhook
- do you want to die bastard? - and cuts his throat.
The last rattle joins the thunder
it is the right spring to die.

A still unripe background
for the appetite of logic
is the cremation sector:
ill-bred pigeons
dogs without a contract
the anarchy of a cat
voices without a throat
crutches, aged bandages,
the Wisdom of the great oven
burns even the soul.

Flessuose manzardine sorridono
prendendo per commedia le urla
di chi le mette in fila per morire
il contorno stesso di quel ridere
è fatto di scenografie spontanee
nuvole disegnate per sembrare lontane
il sipario bruno delle mezzene
e comparse elettrizzate dalla mattana
del regista.

Arriva un cane dal respiro penoso
chi lo finisce?
Nessuno si fa avanti e la bestia
lancia guaiti e domanda ferite
dalla tasca qualcuno estrae la roncola
- vuoi morire bastardo? – e gli taglia la gola.
L'ultimo rantolo si unisce al tuono
è la primavera giusta per morire.

Un retroterra ancora acerbo
per l'appetito della logica
il settore cremazione:
colombi malnati
cani senza contratto
l'anarchia di un gatto
voci prive di gola
stampelle, garze invecchiate,
la Sapienza del grande forno
brucia anche l'anima.

In the pocket of the overalls
I found an eye
who scarifies the heads
remembers and greets me
I hold the eyes for a bit
then feed them to the buzzards.

Of red dawns, here,
we don't feel the neeed
the monotony of the color
thickens the already heavy air,
of scarlet sunsets
let's not talk about those.
Rather the darkness
its complicity
in getting rid of those bony snouts
animalistically eroded by goodness.

Someone asks me if I love
if during the day I search
or I decide, if at least I see.
When they look at my lips
or at my hands
and more mischievously down, between my thighs
I feel the questions on my body
they pass through me
like a pitchfork would do with straw.
If I make the wind bleed
if I transform cold leaves
in meat rolls,
if the white horses of my renaissance
are displayed on the counter of a butcher's shop
I do not renounce my humanity like you
after all.

Nella tasca della tuta
ho trovato un occhio
chi scarnifica le teste
mi ricorda e saluta
gli occhi li tengo un poco
poi ci nutro poiane.

Di albe rosse, qui,
non se ne sente il bisogno
la monotonia del colore
infoltisce l'aria già pesa,
di tramonti vermigli
non parliamone.
Piuttosto il buio
la sua complicità
nel togliere di mezzo quei musi ossuti
animalescamente rosi dalla bontà.

Qualcuno mi chiede se io ami
se durante il giorno cerco
o risolvo, se almeno vedo.
Quando guardano le mie labbra
o le mie mani
e più maliziosamente giù, fra le cosce
sento sul corpo le domande
che mi attraversano
come una forca farebbe con la paglia.
Se faccio sanguinare il vento
se trasformo le foglie fredde
in involtini di carne,
se i cavalli bianchi del mio rinascimento
sono esposti sul bancone di una macelleria
non rinuncio alla mia umanità come voi
del resto.

On a badly colored ocean
a small island floated
the waves spread the origins
the coral chattered at sunset
and the fish re-energized at the well.
It was a drop of sperm
that fell from me into the blood pool
in a morning
of intense slaughter.

Su un oceano colorato malamente
galleggiava una piccola isola
le onde spargevano le origini
i coralli cicalavano al tramonto
e i pesci si rigeneravano alla fonte.
Era una goccia di sperma
cadutami nella vasca del sangue
in una mattina
di forte macellazione.

The Death-Wife
The Imperfect Beasts

This
is the planet of the bright lights
bursts and expands with frantic clarity
the flash of the shot.

The eyes plummet
or rather are lost at the top
where the desire to live
covers the ceiling with wings
for those who fly
it is a friendly day.

They are different cattle
with short hair
thick tufts on the forehead
and light-colored mantles,
the first in the row
receives a hard blow,
once hung it is slaughtered
and he who among us is experienced
takes a paper cup
and tastes the warm blood,
Yugoslavs, he says.

It is an elegant heifer
a spear of straw comes out of her mouth
no premonition
of standing between death and lesser men.

La morte moglie
Le bestie imperfette

Questo
è il pianeta dei bagliori
scoppia e si estende con chiarezza convulsa
il lampo dello sparo.

Gli occhi precipitano
anzi si perdono in alto
dove la voglia di vivere
copre il soffitto di ali
per quelli che volano
è un giorno amico.

Sono bovini diversi
di pelo corto
folti ciuffi sulla fronte
e manti che tendono al chiaro,
il primo della fila
riceve un colpo secco,
una volta appeso lo si sgozza
e chi tra noi ha esperienza
prende un bicchiere di carta
e assaggia il sangue caldo,
jugoslavi, dice.

È una vitella elegante
un filo di paglia le esce dalla bocca
nessun presentimento
di stare tra la morte e uomini minori.

If I broke down the wall of flesh
and hanging from the hook I smiled
what would he say who is paid to dismember
the stamper of tongues
what label would they put on me
how many organs would they discard
and would the vet think panta rei?

The wind
makes a mess of the animals' hair
it is a beastly day
we get on the trucks
we put blankets on their backs
with torturing tenderness.

They lick
the whirling flyes
and the slaughterers,
the iron of the cage
and the pale blue gun.
Then the composed attitude of nature
that has its methods.

A tumor removed
from the liver of the last one killed.
One must know how to recognize
the style of some veterinarians.
They have a gentle touch
they do not tear.
They are the best sellers in the butcher shops.

e sfondassi il muro della carne
e attaccato al gancio sorridessi
cosa direbbe chi è pagato per squartare
il timbratore di lingue
quale etichetta mi metterebbero
quanti organi scarterebbero
e il veterinario penserebbe panta rei?

Il vento
scompiglia i peli delle bestie
è un tempo animale
saliamo sui camion
mettiamo le coperte sui gropponi
con tenerezza aguzzina.

Leccano
i moscerini vertiginosi
e gli abbattitori,
il ferro della gabbia
e la pistola azzurra.
Poi l'aria compita della natura
che ha i suoi metodi.

Asportato un tumore
al fegato dell'ultima uccisa.
Occorre saper riconoscere
lo stile di certi veterinari.
Hanno la mano leggera
non lacerano.
Sono i più venduti nelle macellerie.

I asked the health inspector
if it was possible to save
the sick donkey,
I said that I rarely expressed pity
but the condition of the beast
would have not allowed for stews.
Fearing the worst
the health inspector said that he
for the most part agreed
but the donkey
if he could talk, suicide!

In the center of the hall
the baby colt snorts
in his profile his sentence
to be dirty of mother.

Striking the beast
with more blows
than it can withstand,
sneering
when it realizes
that it is going to die,
giving it the contempt
with the abrasion of a handle
reminding it that its father
its mother, their parents,
its children
its siblings
its own species,
is born
grows and dies [to make us taller.]

Ho chiesto al vigile sanitario
se era possibile salvare
l'asino malato,
ho detto che mi capitava di rado la pietà
ma lo stato della bestia
non avrebbe permesso stracotti.
Temendo il peggio
il vigile sanitario ha detto che lui
per tanta parte era d'accordo
ma l'asino
se avesse avuto la parola, suicidio!

Al centro della sala
il piccolo puledro soffia
al suo profilo la sua pena
essere sporco di madre.

Dare alla bestia
più botte
di quante ne regga,
ghignare
quando si rende conto
che sta per morire,
dargli il disprezzo
di una abrasione da manico,
ricordargli che il padre
la madre, i genitori di entrambi,
i figli
i fratelli
la specie sua,
è nata
cresciuta e morta [per renderci più alti.]

Relationships don't belong here
but the withered grass of the stable does
(it changes often).
No heart is ashamed to glimpse
a piece of butt
and the designated range of equally supreme gestures
does not break.

The dying beast
agonizes alone
because no thing
happens held in the arms.

Larger
than pain is the universe
that from afar seems so vast
and yellow like the paper
that wraps pieces of cheap cut
low-quality beef.

One day
that I hoped was a holiday
I myself shouted
I am lamb too.

Non c'entrano i rapporti
ma l'erba appassita della stalla
(si cambia spesso).
Nessun cuore ha vergogna di adocchiare
parte del culo
e non si spezza l'ampiezza designata dei gesti
ugualmente supremi.

La bestia morente
agonizza da sola
perché nessuna cosa
avviene tra le braccia.

Più grande
del dolore è l'universo
che da lontano sembra così vasto
e giallo come la carta
che avvolge i pezzi di carne povera
la bassa macelleria.

Un giorno
che speravo fosse festa
io stesso gridavo
sono agnello anch'io.

The word
feels sought by the beasts, it
can say that the eternal lasts
one day at most,
and the pillows[1] are not storage
for hesitant dreams.

Counting worms
in spoiled and abandoned meat
the lawn on the side (external east)
each with its own numbers
far from this world here
like the buzz
of the saw cutting in half
a quarter and voilà.

With dozens of hits
we have crushed the last head
one respects the schedule not the method
like when into the ground
the frost settles the issue.

Nobody asks anymore questions
dozens of carcasses are ready
the expedient of work shifts doesn't matter
the answers must be loaded.

---

1   The Italian "guanciale" means both "pillow" and a common cut of meat called "pork jowl" in English. "Pillow" was chosen for the translation because it better conveys the presence of an object that can "store dreams".

La parola
si sente cercata dalle bestie, lei
sa dire che l'eterno dura
al massimo un giorno,
e i guanciali non sono depositi
di sogni esitanti.

La conta dei vermi
nella carne guasta e abbandonata
prato a latere (esterno est)
ciascuno con i suoi numeri
distanti da questo mondo qua
come il ronzio
della sega che taglia a mezzo
un quarto e voilà.

Con decine di colpi
abbiamo frantumato l'ultima testa
si rispetta l'orario non la misura
come dentro la terra
il gelo chiude la questione.

Nessuno fa più domande
decine di carcasse sono pronte
non conta l'espediente dei turni
bisogna caricare le risposte.

You all are the host species,
it was told me by the one who in the vet's book
is called platyhelminthes cestoda
with segmented body,
that hides inside pork.

In the race between ascaris (tapeworms in horses)
a cigarette is the start
matches are the finish line,
the more you cut the tapeworm the more it moves
snip, snip
and each piece runs independently
someone cheers for the chosen segment
others help it with their hand.

I rip out
the silent heart
of a young bull
and I offer it
to his lesser gods.

At what distance are the innards
I in the bowels very slowly
so small and warm
in my hand
death.

La specie ospite siete voi,
me lo ha detto colui che sul libro del veterinario
è chiamato platelminta cestode
dal corpo nastriforme,
che si nasconde nella carne di maiale.

Nella gara tra ascaridi (tenie di cavallo)
una sigaretta è la partenza
i minerva il traguardo,
la tenia più la tagli e più si muove
zac, zac
e ogni pezzo corre per suo conto,
qualcuno incita il segmento scelto
altri lo aiutano con la mano.

Strappo
il cuore silenzioso
di un torello
e lo offro
ai suoi dèi modesti.

A che distanza sono le interiora
io nel ventre piano piano
così piccola e calda
in mano mia
la morte.

Who spread this
farfetched rumor
that animals are prejudiced
against me?

An ox
bumps into a barrel of fat
in this way reason breaks
and the body rises.

Extremely long and narrow knife
two people hold her
a third one hands hay,
surrounded by good intentions
the beast calms down, eats
even from the hand of a man,
suddenly a fourth figure
approaches from behind
with one glimpse he calculates the position
between head and neck as they say
gently points the knife and pushes
with all his strength.
The beast collapses
opening wide her white
eyes.

Chi ha messo in giro questa
diceria inaudita
che su di me vi siano pregiudizi
da parte delle bestie?

Un bue
urta contro un barile di grasso
così si spezza la ragione
e insorge il corpo.

Coltello lunghissimo e stretto
due persone la tengono
una terza porge fieno,
circondata da buone intenzioni
la bestia si calma, mangia
addirittura nella mano dell'uomo,
all'improvviso una quarta figura
si avvicina da dietro
con uno sguardo calcola la posizione
tra testa e collo come si dice
punta delicatamente il coltello e spinge
con tutta la sua forza.
La bestia crolla
strabuzzando gli occhi
bianchi.

On Labor Day
we are more than fifty
executioners, rippers
who slaughter and who collect blood
meat trimmers, skinners, movers
those who slaughter door-to-door
tanners, packers and gravediggers,
the working class.

A Scottish calf
must heal before dying.
This mesh of fine meat
has a secret that must be respected.
Only the lungs thrown away.

As hard as clotted blood
and as soft as calf's marrow
similar am I if not equal.

Snout against snout
they exchange tongues
licking each other's smile
the pregnant beasts
the rest of their bodies is
made of crag and glass.

Il primo maggio
siamo più di cinquanta
boia, squartatori
chi sgozza e chi raccoglie il sangue
trippai, scuoiatori, facchini
quelli che macellano a domicilio
pellai, insaccatori e necrofori,
la classe operaia.

Un vitellone scozzese
deve guarire prima di morire.
Questa trama di carne pregiata
ha un segreto che va rispettato.
Buttati solo i polmoni.

Duro come sangue rappreso
e morbido come il midollo di un vitello
sono così se non addirittura uguale.

Muso contro muso
si scambiano le lingue
ciascuna lecca il suo sorriso
le bestie gravide
sono in tutto il resto del corpo
di rupe e di vetro.

The calves don't let themselves be touched
even by the voice,
the edible meat
is in full bloom.

The sun rises
in its youngest sky
the light first vacillates
then shines on the knives.

A yellow butterfly with black stripes
lands on the hand of the slaughterer
he touches her with a puff of air and she leaves
towards other ways of dying.

I vitelloni non si fanno toccare
neanche con la voce,
la carne alimentare
è in pieno fiore.

Il sole sorge
nel suo più giovane cielo
la luce prima vacilla
poi brilla sui coltelli.

Una farfalla gialla con righe nere
si posa sulla mano di chi sgozza
lui la sfiora con un soffio e lei va via
verso altri modi di morire.

The Death-Wife

to Luciana Cappi

You sign
moving your fingers like claws
these are simple days of agony
you have phlebitis
the maker of the body cannot be consoled
you lie on a large table about to be eaten.

Help, help
the word is picked clean and there is no silence,
it's me writing,
help, help
you stain my veins with ink
and you are the end of every name.

You have inside
the uncertainty of the return
I tell you what you have to do
cling to every silent form
look around as you do in the bathroom
find a shadow and its grip on the skin
you have been scattered and accelerated
the mirror can be cold
busy with other harmonies.

La morte moglie

A Luciana Cappi

Fai segni
oscillando le dita a graffio
sono giorni semplici di agonia
hai la flebite
il fabbricatore del corpo non si dà pace
stai su una grande tavola per essere mangiata.

Aiuto, aiuto
si spolpa la parola e non c'è silenzio,
sono io che sto scrivendo,
aiuto, aiuto
macchi d'inchiostro le mie vene
e sei la fine di ogni nome.

Hai dentro
l'incertezza del ritorno
ti dico quello che devi fare
aggrappati a ogni forma silenziosa
guardati intorno come fai nel bagno
trova un'ombra e la sua morsa sulla pelle
sei stata diffusa e accellerata
lo specchio può essere gelido
impegnato in altre armonie.

Stripped
as it is of all goods
the light arrives
you are alone and you look like the universe
that has been picking its black holes for hours.

It's so sober this season
and wise this winter
that the adventure is tame
and doomed. I owe
the eternity of a bite to your tongue
a kiss that arises soft.

That kiss
actually hurried us
although it was not summer and spring
winter and fall
not even in the sensitivity of the taste bud
there was an alarm
the cataclysms happened earlier
and the deities were praised
this action of flight and thirst remained
gone extinct with the vials.

Spoglia
com'è di ogni bene
arriva la luce
sei sola e sembri l'universo
che scaccola da ore i suoi buchi neri.

È così sobria la stagione
e saggio questo inverno
che l'avventura è mite
e condannata. Devo
l'eternità di un morso alla tua lingua
un bacio che insorga leggero.

Quel bacio
in realtà ci mise fretta
benché non fosse estate e primavera
inverno e autunno
se nemmeno nella sensibilità della papilla
ci fosse allarme
i cataclismi fossero anteriori
e le divinità lodate
restava questa azione di fuga e sete
estinta con le fiale.

Behind the cured beef
a little before the tenderloin
after the horse steak
to the left of the prosciutto
to the right of the cooked ham
in front of the parmesan and over the jam
is a pack of "ready to eat"
Roland anchovies.

Pseudo fusilli pasta
animistic vegetables
your surging snout on the mezzaluna knife
chopping and chopping again the gracious passage
nothing can be done except a meal
this is the loot of the human struggle.

I wander in the lukewarm soup
you are bothered by my slow mouth
that lingers on bile-colored vegetables
drops fall from between my teeth
splashes, unstoppable slurps, la merde
c'est ma cuisinière.

You were so godly
and timely
to transport yourself
to this human stratum
following the song
of les bananettes.

Dietro la bresaola
un po' prima del filetto
dopo la scottona di cavallo
a sinistra del prosciutto crudo
a destra del cotto
di fronte al grana e oltre le marmellate
c'è una confezione di "pronto a tavola"
alici Riunione.

Simil fusilli
animistiche verdure
il tuo muso ondoso sulla mezzaluna
trita e ritrita il transito cortese
niente si può se non un pasto
questo è il bottino della lotta umana.

Vagabondo nella minestra tiepida
sei spazientita dalla mia bocca lenta
che indugia su verdure color fiele
escono dalle stretture dei denti gocce
scrosci, imprendibili risucchi, la merde
c'est ma cuisinière.

Tu quanto dio
e tempestivo fosti
per deportarti
in questo tratto umano
seguendo il canto
delle bananettes.

In the act
of licking the palm of the hand
immersed in the folds of the liberty style blanket
isolated from any affection and therefore in the early morning
when the sheet tilts and the day becomes athletic
the slow steps of the breath
illuminate like ghosts a blind spot
the pale emptiness of the paper.

You don't have the face
you had an hour ago
your features moved
it is a matter of pulling out every word
from the flesh
to tell what makes a man's mouth water.

Oh God forgive this instinct as a final goal
and the melancholic crew of these lullabies,
a light breath settles on the white curtains
the child's ball ended in the shit
the child asks the shit for his ball.

I have a dream
where the minotaur is a whole person
Pasiphae
twinkles branch out through the night
gnomes, lemurs, unicorns rise up here and there.

Nell'atto
di leccare il palmo della mano
immerse nelle pieghe liberty della coperta
fuori da ogni bene e dunque di primo mattino
quando reclina il foglio e il giorno diventa atletico
i lenti passi del respiro
illuminano spettrali un punto orbo
il vuoto smorto della carta.

Non hai la faccia
che avevi un'ora fa
i lineamenti si sono mossi
si tratta di staccare ogni parola
dalla carne
per dire cosa fa gola a un uomo.

Oddio perdona l'istinto come meta
e il malinconico equipaggio di queste cantilene,
un leggero fiato si posa sulle tende bianche
la palla del bambino è andata sulla merda
il bambino chiede palla alla merda.

I have a dream
laddove il minotauro sia una persona intera
Pasifae
la notte è rameggiata dai brillii
gnomi, lemuri, liocorni insorgono qua e là.

Evil
so openly trickles
that the wait is gathering inside the house
see how her face is moon-like
an aluminum shroud
kisses her on her pain.

The eyes plummet
or rather are lost at the top
where the desire to live
covers the ceiling with wings.

It's the movement of the lazy crisis
tongues explode from mouth to mouth
every technique generates a mystic
between bedpans and vials
Fetonte's misdeed enters the final trail
an act of sabotage of the resurrection.

So you don't care about
the open "e" in Valeria
it was just a way to feel hurt
and so dream for me the change
the pronunciation of her alone.

Il male
tanto apertamente cola
che nella casa si raduna attesa
vedi com'è di luna il viso
un velo d'alluminio
la bacia sul dolore.

Gli occhi precipitano
anzi si perdono in alto
dove la voglia di vivere
copre il soffitto di ali.

È il movimento della crisi pigra
da bocca a bocca esplodono le lingue
ogni tecnica genera una mistica
tra comode e flaconi
la gabazza di Fetonte tenta la carraia finale
pratica gappista della resurrezione.

Non ti interessa dunque
la e aperta di Valeria
era solo un modo di dolerti
e allora sognami il cambiamento
la pronuncia di lei soltanto.

Staggered by light
when you finish radiotherapy
reason becomes a sentimental act of revolt
and a kiss is the abstract art of the mouth
there is a slow entrance of manners
madeleine brigade.

A trophy of seasons is left
the childlike reptilianness of the living
without knowing how to distinguish a terrestrial
from a fresh-aquatic
a lepidosaur from a scaled one.

Light was touching you and I did the same
on the walls and in the sighs of the shadows
little clandestine wonders
you were going elsewhere and that's why
we blushed for a kiss,
Psyche who volunteers to guard
Cupid dies a bigot.

You are the substance that converts me
that bleeds docile in the eyes
the shadow has gone out
the body instead pirouettes in the air
and as if they had a single mind they pursue
two or three wild flowers
yet fear isn't anything complete
peace contains nothing.

Si barcolla di luce
quando esci dalla radioterapia
la ragione diventa un atto sentimentale di rivolta
e un bacio l'arte astratta della bocca
c'è una lenta imboccatura della maniera
brigata madeleine.

Resta un trofeo di stagioni
la rettilitudine bambina di chi vive
senza saper distinguere un terrestre da un dulcacquicolo
un lepidosauro da uno squamato.

La luce ti toccava e io con lei
sui muri e nei sospiri delle ombre
piccole meraviglie clandestine
te ne andavi altrove e per questo
si arrossiva per un bacio,
Psiche che si presta alla guardia
di Amore perisce settaria.

Sei tu la materia che mi converte
che sanguine docile negli occhi
si è spenta l'ombra
il corpo invece piroetta in aria
e come avessero una testa sola inseguono
due o tre fiori domenicali
eppure la paura non è niente di intero
la pace non contiene nulla.

I don't know how to pray
tremors and glimpses of anxiety grow
in the ravine of the bed
in the cleaning of opaqueness always an uncharted space.
Never again the materialism of the hinges
but the little flute that whistles in the chest
and gives an extra euphoria to the night.

You play and cry
you don't say anything and don't even listen
spring
the end.

Knowing how to beastly talk about the fleet
of hands that speak the gesture
from the last caress to the icy sea of the skin
- rose water, rose water -
life is no longer a shared space
now I enter and swallow up entire ponds of pain
in the ground fog of breaths that is compassion.

Here is the simple day when we existed
now we do not even know
who made us cry and what to do with this gasp
without hope of breathing.

Non so pregare
crescono tremori e scorci d'ansia
nel burrone del letto
nella pulizia dell'opaco sempre inesplorato spazio.
Mai più il materialismo delle cerniere
ma lo zuffolotto che nel petto pispola
e dà alla notte una fischiarella in più.

Giochi e piangi
non dici nulla e nemmeno ascolti
la primavera
fine.

Saper dire bestialmente della flotta
di mani che pronunciano il gesto
dall'ultima carezza al mare gelido della pelle
– acqua di rosa, acqua di rosa –
il luogo comune non è più la vita
ora entro e risucchio interi stagni di dolore
nella bassa nebbia di fiati che è la compassione.

Ecco il giorno semplice che siamo stati
ora nemmeno sappiamo
chi ci ha fatto piangere e cosa fare di questo fiato
senza speranza di respiro.

Removed from the mind every purpose of form
in the amniotic darkness of the bed flow
reticent outcrops of light,
the bleeding blue of the surfaces
creates small clusters of human havoc
tiny vortices.

She swallows quickly
I alternate between fast and ill-suited flights
the precision of the unknown is here
look at that untamed figure crushing
the habit of dying.

Your eyes are locked on the dismissed
which in every scandal is natural
so look me right in the face
living as the dead is not difficult.

Tiny corpse
want to exhaust the experience of guilt
come onto the pebbles of pain
I ask her for a glass of geocentric gelatin
a decubitus of existence
without wasting away with funeral songs or
buzzing relationships with the sky.

Tolto dal pensiero ogni scopo di forma
nel buio amniotico del letto scorrono
affioramenti taciturni di luce,
il sanguinante azzurro delle superfici
crea piccoli gnocchi di soqquadro umano
vorticini.

Rapida deglutisce
io mi alterno a voli rapidi e inadatti
c'è la precisione dell'ignoto
guarda che brado schiacciamento di figura
l'abitudine a morire.

Hai gli occhi fissi sul dimesso
che in ogni scandalo è naturale
allora guardami bene in faccia
vivere da morti non è difficile.

Morticina
voglia esaurire l'esperienza delle colpe
venga sui ciottoletti di dolore
le chiedo un bicchierotto di gelatina geocentrica
un decubito d'esistenza
senza sciuparsi con ariette funeree o ronzii
di relazione con il cielo.

The outcome
germinates sacredly awake
there is no need for the splendor of the Oriflamme
the day leaves definitively
I am the one without the ticket
you the ship's figurehead with the tumor.

The wind
ruffles the few hairs on the head
it yelps and growls it shakes off and gets us wet.
Let's shut the window...

You are destined to fluctuation and I myself
fly over the gray gleam of the air
so in the mist the solitary wholeness of the flesh
is annihilated by the image
furious Ludd and hyper-driven love.

Sooner or later
the places will disappear
the names will come back
the shadow puppetry will replace the light
concave and convex exhaustion
will invade our cheeks with shit and granite
and the last breath of history will be drawn with soup.

L'esito
germoglia destamente sacro
non c'è bisogno del fulgore d'orifiamma
il giorno parte definitivamente
io sono quello che non ha il biglietto
tu la polena col tumore.

Il vento
scompiglia i peli della testa
guaisce e ringhia si scrolla e ci bagna.
Chiudiamo la finestra...

Sei destinata alla fluttuazione e io stesso
sorvolo il barlume grigio dell'aria
così nella nebbia la pienezza solitaria della carne
si annienta nel sembiante
Ludd furente e ipertrainato amore.

Prima o poi
i luoghi scompariranno
ritorneranno indietro i nomi
il teatro delle ombre sostituirà la luce
concave e convesse sfinitezze
ci invaderanno le guance di merda e di granito
e il fiato della storia esalerà dei consommé.

It announces phonemes
by making black tongues rain
there is god in the cleft lip of heaven
now it comes down
breaks through the mouths of the houses
steals death rattles from the chest
scrapes the crying in the throat
establishes itself in a Hamletic state.

The terror that I have of the word
of its hard foliage
of its torment headed up toward elsewhere
ready to tattoo shadows inside extreme dimples
to visit my chest with needles of lines.

They explained that there is a mass
that compresses the tragic
this mass makes you regress to simply
help me clear out shit from my heart.

Moist sky
that expands and contracts
among the gibbets of Villon, the greek tragedies of Racine
and the enamel urinal.
Slaps of water are sailing
a conscious effusion of withering
greenish and yellow liquid nothingness
I will dry it in the verse like a longshoreman.

Annuncia fonemi
facendo piovere lingue nere
c'è dio nel labbro leporino del cielo
ora scende giù
sfonda le bocche delle case
ruba dal petto i rantoli
raspa nella gola il pianto
si costituisce in stato amletico.

Terrore che ho della parola
del suo fogliame duro
del suo tormento a scala verso altrove
pronta a tatuare ombre dentro fossette estreme
a visitarmi il petto con gli aghi delle righe.

Hanno spiegato che c'è una massa
che comprime il tragico
questa massa ti fa regredire al semplice
aiutami a sgombrare merda dal cuore.

Cielo umido
che si espande e contrae
tra le forche di Villon, le greche di Racine
e l'orinale di smalto.
Veleggiano schiaffoni d'acqua
una effusione conscia della sfioritura
nulla liquido verdino e giallo
l'asciugherò nel verso come un camallo.

It is sunset
enough change for her
since death is born every day.

The illegitimate nature of flies
the rancor in their logical revolts
this enormous crowd of raw meat
toxic apotheosis of the inner man.

However
the human race
appears and frees itself
in the tears
norms lunatic voices
that carry the veil.

Did you see that future times venture into facial features?
They will end by hermetic combustion
on the broad forehead of our poaching.

This is the time for transparency
the statuesque mechanics of light
illuminate the urine bag
human finishing touches and dyed decorations.

È tramonto
le basta come cambiamento
dato che la morte nasce ogni giorno.

La natura illegittima delle mosche
il rancore nelle loro rivolte logiche
questa folla immensa di carne cruda
apoteosi tossica dell'uomo interiore.

Tuttavia
la razza umana
si accenna e si affranca
nelle lacrime
norme lunatiche voci
che portano il velo.

Hai visto che i futuri azzardano lineamenti?
Finiranno per combustion ermetica
sulla fronte ampia del nostro bracconaggio.

Questa è l'ora delle trasparenze
la statuaria meccanica della luce
illumina la sacca dell'urina
rifiniture umane e addobbi tinti.

The bed goes up and down
with a screech that is music and rapture
like certain childish songs
voices that change the weight of the universe
in the transient and laxative idea
of the beautiful complexion of your silence.

I wished I had shaken off
the dust of the exploded statues
to give myself to the winners cleaned up
but there is no place that remains whole
nor century with any time left
it dies it is dying matter
enormous shadow of the alphabet.

Entering into your oblique gaze
feeling neither the soul nor the divine phosphorus
but only the cold tip of bones and the skin
surrendered to your profile. This awakening
even during the day spends the night and waits for repatriation
it brings to mind the way toads
kiss large spans of sky:
the stars, the stars!

In the dancing circle of wonder
everything that dozes acts
today the internship of shitting on sight
unloaded! they scream happily.

Il letto si alza e si abbassa
in uno stridio che è musica e rapina
come certe cantilene infantili
voci che cambiano peso all'universo
nell'idea transitoria e lassativa
della bella cera del tuo silenzio.

Avrei voluto scrollarmi di dosso
la polvere delle statue esplose
offrendomi ripulito ai vincitori
ma non c'è luogo che rimanga intero
né secolo a cui resti tempo
muore sta morendo la materia
enorme ombra d'alfabeto.

Entrare nel tuo sguardo obliquo
senza sentire né anima né fosforo divino
ma solo la punta fredda delle ossa e la pelle
arresa al tuo profilo. Questo risveglio
pernotta anche il giorno e aspetta il rimpatrio
viene in mente il modo che hanno i rospi
di baciare grandi spanne di cielo:
le stelle, le stelle!

Nel ballotondo della meraviglia
tutto quello che sonnecchia agisce
oggi il tirocinio di cagare a vista
scaricata! urlano allegramente.

With archival flair
the light of the landscape swings
the tactical temptation of dreams creates a curtain
the topographical convention of meaning dances
we fall in love with sleep.

How the language bleeds now
in the word stuck in our throats
the same coming and going without doing
to sheathe ourselves in the conversion.

We experience the glowing order of separation
the onset of the present in the flesh
here the knowledge of pain occurs
the unknown dimension of amazement.

Every word
is an archaeological find
peel the first layer, the second, the third
what remains is a useless thing from thousands of years ago
often poetry collects dust
and reveals that it is essential to show oneself dead
there is more intensity and desire in the end
than in the posture of the text.

Con estro d'archivio
dondola la luce del paesaggio
la tentazione tattica dei sogni crea sipario
danza la convenzione topografica del senso
ci si innamora del sonno.

Come sanguina il linguaggio ora
nella parola che si pianta in gola
lo stesso andare e venire senza fare
per invaginarsi nella conversione.

Viviamo l'ordine raggiante del distacco
l'insorgenza del presente nella carne
qui avviene il sapere del dolore
la misura ignota dello stupore.

Ogni parola
è un reperto archeologico
via il primo strato, il secondo, il terzo
ciò che resta è una cosa inutile di migliaia di anni fa
spesse volte la poesia accumula polvere
e rivela che è indispensabile mostrarsi morti
c'è più intensità e desiderio nella fine
che nel portamento del testo.

From whom should I save you
if you die inside the same atoms
and crack different verdicts
is not healthy this earthly multitude made
of a single beauty.
This night your profile
has some unholy and mystical attitudes
your thinning hair like an angel in its gloomy appearance
you are dreaming of being separated from the dream.

The opportunities to withdraw are over
the horizon is lying at your side
and the sun makes noise no longer.

Like paper
you rise to the eyes until you are ashes
then you close the window
before the sedatives learn the night
poetry like the revolution is never romantic
it burns the distance of saying goodbye
yet the noise of the verse does not lack amazement
there is an underlayer of ravines and starry skies
in the chanting of the gravel on the tomb.

Da chi devo salvarti
se muori dentro gli stessi atomi
e schiocchi altre pronunce
non è sana questa terrena moltitudine
di una bellezza sola.
Questa notte il tuo profilo
ha degli atteggiamenti irreligiosi e mistici
i capelli radi come un angelo nel suo aspetto cupo
sogni di essere separata dal sogno.

Le occasioni per arretrare sono finite
si corica al tuo fianco l'orizzonte
e il sole non fa più rumore.

Simile alla carta
insorgi agli occhi fino a farti cenere
poi chiudi la finestra
prima che i sedative imparino la notte
la poesia come la rivoluzione non è mai amorosa
brucia la misura del dirsi addio
eppure non manca lo stupore al frastuono del verso
c'è un sottosuolo di voragini e firmamenti
nella cantafera della ghiaia sulla tomba.